Fragile Body Fragile Mind
What's the Difference?

by B.Gilzene

Illustrated by Makalia McKenzie

Acknowledgement

This book is dedicated to supportive family and friends and especially to the young man called Jermaine who I met in Wood Green, north London on 14th November 2013. His humility and kindness saved me.

CONTENTS

1 The Nightmare

2 Been there!

3 The Unlikely Samaritan

4 The Valuable Advice

5 Self- Reflection

The Nightmare

The Nightmare

Emma stood at the bus stop in the rain unable to use the folded umbrella she always carried.

"Come here!" a mother said angrily to her inquisitive little girl.

"But mummy---" the girl responded whilst being dragged away.

Three buses arrived at the same time after a twenty minute wait.

Those waiting in the queue in front of Emma boarded in order, one after the other. Those in the queue behind overtook her and got on, some gently nudging her as they did so.

Emma finally boarded the bus.

Sighs and "Come on hurry up," in loud and low voices were heard amongst the passengers waiting to depart.

Emma just needed a little bit of time to retrieve her purse, pay her fare and to find a seat, all of which were occupied.

Arriving at her destination, the driver opened the doors. Emma was standing nearby so began to exit. Just as before, those behind her, some with sighs, others, with under breath comments, impatiently alighted before she could.

*

At the Post Office there was a long queue and only three cashiers serving.

Unruly toddlers carelessly ran around. Unlike the old days no one corrected their behaviour to prevent any possible accidents. Not the seemingly oblivious parent, the security guard or any of the irritated waiting customers.

Some thirty minutes later the cashier spoke very loudly to Emma causing the chatting customers to become silent, even the unruly toddlers were suddenly still and observant.

Emma, in her own time left the Post Office without the impatient responses as before.

*

The supermarket appeared much larger than usual. Fortunately it was not busy. The carrier bag, not particularly heavy was cumbersome.

As Emma walked towards the bus stop, she tried to ignore the ceased conversations of the couples and groups and their one by one stares, as well as the loud and hushed whispers, of those standing about and those who stepped widely past her.

On another occasion Emma had felt something, which was followed by laughers. It sounded like an empty drink can as it bounced off of her, down to the pavement.

At the encouragement of parents' prejudices, young children ran past Emma's house, scared. They did not know why they were scared.

These unwarranted experiences sometimes made Emma feel sad, sometimes angry, and on very few occasions, like lashing out, forcing her to distance herself.

*

At home all was calm - an environment in which Emma could share, rest and weep, with family and friends, who accepted her unconditionally and where she could do whatever she wanted in her own time without being abused and patronised. Here, Emma felt warm, safe, loved, respected and happy.

*

Six weeks later at her local hospital, Emma sat patiently, reading an outdated magazine, occasionally glancing at her ticket. She was number 27. Although the wait was long, she was pleased that her number was not say, 49, otherwise it would've been dark and more people in the street and on the buses travelling from work by the time she left the hospital. Crowds, especially unkind ones made Emma feel uneasy.

"Emma Butterworth. Emma Butterworth." The almost inaudible call caused Emma to replace the magazine and rise from her seat as quickly as she could. She had just about heard her name amongst the busyness of the waiting area.

Imagine if she hadn't, she'd have to wait all over again for another appointment for the next week or month.

"Hello Emma"

"Hello doctor."

"Sit down. That's it. How have you been? How's your leg?"

"Oh doctor, I'm just so glad the plaster's coming off today. It's been a nightmare!"

Been there!

Amongst others, I read, 'One Day My Soul Just Opened Up' by Iyanla Vanzant and felt relief when I read the introduction, 'Removing the Veil.' It could have been about me. As it happened I had taken time out of a twenty year career. I, like Iyanla experienced feelings of misery, confusion, and despair. I even became combative, on a train and a bus, which on each occasion were full of passengers.

Anyway, I needed to take the time out; otherwise I would have been sacked, carted off to a psychiatric ward or even assassinated.

My body, like a pressure cooker with its years of eclectic experiences and emotions simmered, boiled, then as the 'heat' was not turned down, exploded – releasing the steam of life.

For a while I was in denial – trying to fool myself that I couldn't possibly be insane.

*

I travelled through the psychological process of recalling past events, some good and some not so good. During these periods, it was difficult to focus on the positives in my life.

After feeling that all toddlers and overweight people were out to get me, and later, urges to slapping, anyone in sight as I walked down the street, I was forced to acknowledge that I had to do something and urgently.

The first thing I did was to remain within the confines of my home, occasionally going out to the shops. The people I ignored as I did so, didn't realise how fortunate they were. I didn't have the capacity to be friendly and I didn't want to take any chances.

I accepted that I had crossed over the thin line, so got myself a therapist, who stated I was 'over stressed.' Thinking that I was insane had at least prompted me to address whatever was causing my strange state of mind and behaviour.

The therapy sessions were difficult, as I was forced to confront myself, and experiences, which included illogical phobias.

Some revelations were better than others. There were times when I realised I had hurt a lot of people, such as when I had hunted down an ex, armed with a knife.

These sessions were not confined to the therapy room; I continued to self-reflect, and to accept the changes occurring within me - the changes which included understanding and letting go.

I now understand, for example, that my frustration with those with power was due to my lack of power, and inability to feed the hungry, shelter the homeless, stop all wars, and all forms of exploitation, which I had blamed others for. I had blamed them for my powerlessness to make things better.

My fear of lively toddlers related to when mine were, and the overwhelming responsibility of protecting them which became almost impossible as I only have two eyes. As for my phobia about overweight people, this was suppressed anger relating to criticisms about my natural thinness.

No amount of explanation would have been accepted if I had acted on my urges to slap - "Oh I'm terribly sorry. I slapped you because I've only just realised that my ex had been cheating on me longer than I'd initially thought, or; I'm terribly sorry but I'm still angry that I didn't get promoted after doing the job for almost eight years and those I trained those who came after me had, or; I'm terribly sorry but I was not believed when I was wrongly accused of stealing...."

I was lucky, and feel for those, who have carried out their urges because they had not received the support which may have prevented them from doing so. (Perhaps some murders, for example, may have been prevented if appropriate support had been accessed in time).

*

It's funny but I feel calm and at peace, since I've been true to myself. Being 'insane' isn't as bad as I thought. In fact it's a kind of relief. I'm relieved from being compliant to what I never really felt comfortable with, such as some of the government and religious rules, just to be accepted as 'normal,' by psychopathic predators. I'm released from living up to the expectations of others.

How can being restricted and forced to being someone you're not be 'normal'?

For me, being normal is to be liberated – releasing spirituality, truth, acceptance, choice, forgiveness, realising what's important, and becoming unafraid of new experiences and challenges - To think 'outside of the box'. Now I think of it, my own experience of 'insanity' had awakened me!

I've been called mad, a witch, even Satan, which I don't mind because I feel true and at peace with myself - better than when I was 'sensible' and compliant just to 'fit in,' which I never really did anyway.

I'm now satisfied with what I have – a family, smaller selection of friends, a home and a battered, but reliable car. They're all ok. I'm ok. I also have the confidence to do what I have always wanted to do, instead of getting stressed and frustrated thinking about it.

My mantra is 'Everything happens for a reason and nothing happens before the time' as well as, 'Trust and Obey God's Will.

Convenient? Urrh, yes! lyanla, no, the Divine she refers to, has verified that this is ok. Anyway my renewed self, influenced by her and TD Jakes and most importantly, Jermaine, (apologies if I have misspelt your name) a homeless young person, as I was on my way to a therapy session, helped.

Shame I won't recognise Jermaine if I saw him again as I have a condition called Prosopagnosia - an inability to recognise people by their faces, but that's another story!

*

When I returned to work, I wondered if I had done sooner than I should have. Fortunately being able to work from home was convenient on the occasions I felt overwhelmed.

I'm now doing what this life long journey has been preparing me to do, and at the risk of sounding like James Brown, I feel good!

The Unlikely Samaritan

The Unlikely Samaritan

Apparently in the old days doctors used to say to those with what we know as depression, or more recently, 'emotional stress' "Stop feeling sorry for yourself!
Pull yourself together!
Life is what you make it.....!"

*

Whilst at work her mobile vibrated. Not recalling the train journey she was home in no time.

Her husband and his mother, who was the one who had contacted her, were home.
It was difficult for her to comprehend the new situation; in which she had found herself – the situation they had all now found themselves. It was so sudden, so unexpected, so unpredictable, so...

*

He was a teacher and enjoyed being so, including the increasing changes and challenges, which he seemed to thrive on. Then all of a sudden he felt there was something missing from his life. Out of the blue he had this 'Reach for the Sky' mentality and started attending various money making conferences which were held in plush central London hotels and facilitated by charismatic twenty and thirty something year olds wearing expensive suits and enticing delegates to believe that they too could be as rich as they were, if not richer, enabling free, independent and fun filled life styles.

Influenced, he succumbed and did very well – purchasing products, and introducing people to them. Those people then purchased the products and introduced other people, and so the chain continued. He admitted that this was as hard as teaching a class of teenagers, but the financial gains were better.

He continued to teach and in a short space of time was managing large amounts of people in his new business, many of whom he did not know.

After work he regularly attended meetings and facilitated conferences in London hotels. He was doing very well and so relinquished his teaching career to focus solely on the business.

As the saying goes, *nothing lasts forever*. After a year the business went bust. He and many others lost their investments. That was when he went into, a 'Big Sulk'.

*

Days and weeks passed he refused to speak, wash and on occasions, eat and sleep – sometimes pacing the floor day and night. His interchangeable moods were difficult to cope with. They included happiness and optimism, sadness, aggression, laughter and cursing - to himself or his 'invisible friend' as well as to those who loved and cared about him. He refused to leave the spare room, let alone the house, which was a blessing in disguise as, who knows what would have happened to him and possibly to others.

After weeks, then months of walking on eggshells, and trying to anticipate how she should respond if---- she decided she'd had enough and eventually said without fear or guilt, “So you lost the business. Stop feeling for sorry yourself. Pull yourself together!” It was a risk she felt she had to take.

The following day he emerged, sporting a beard, untidy hair, unbrushed teeth and an unpleasant body odour, from the spare room which he had occupied for almost three months.

*

The days and months went by when she returned home from her now part-time work to care for him, which was shared with his mother. The tasks included, supporting and encouraging him to eat, drink, bathe, take prescribed medication, relearn personal and social skills. She was also on guard and prepared for any unpredictable behaviour.

*

After some months he eventually came out from his ‘Big Sulk’ and resumed work as a Supply Teacher.

Like everyone else, he sometimes gets in a mood and sulks, but not like when he was unwell - had crashed - had a breakdown – was emotionally stressed; However it is described, it was an illness and like any other illness, needed medical or another kind of assistance, as well as affection, kindness and patience to aid recovery.

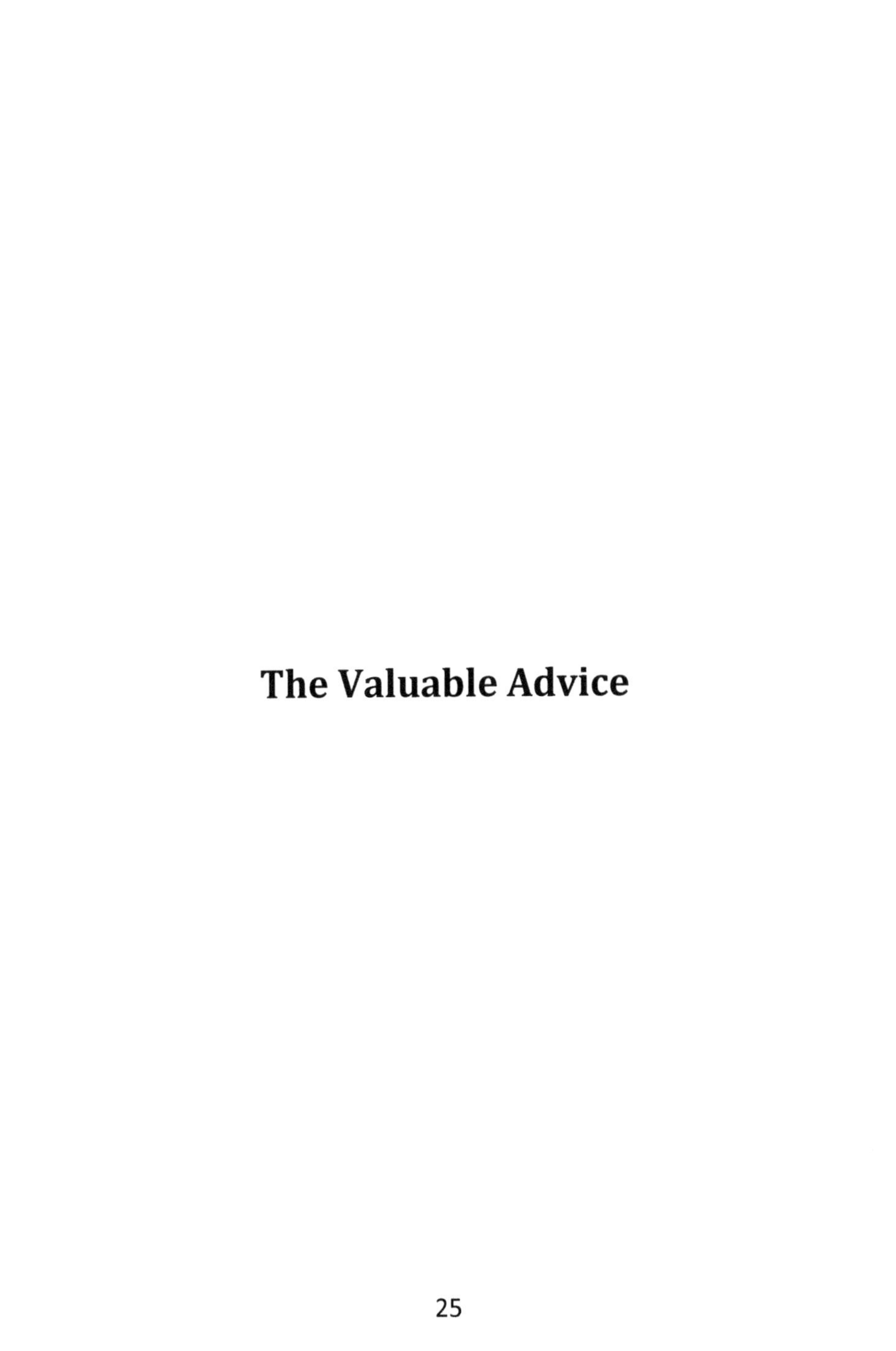

The Valuable Advice

The Valuable Advice

"Oh luv, you look exhausted. Come and sit down," said Violet tapping the vacant seat next to her. The mother, she was addressing was parking the buggy with one hand which had almost tipped over due to loaded shopping bags on its handles. She was also carrying a screaming toddler.

Close to the parked buggy with its sleeping new-born, the mother took up the seat.

Taking in the pleasantness of the old woman's' face, the toddler's screams ceased. He stared as she communicated to him in his language.

"You need to be careful. Look after yuself, so you can look after them kiddies. Take it from me love." The old woman told the mother in an adult voice.

"I was a wife, mother, nurse, cook, cleaner, maid. You name it, I dun it. I dun everyfink." She continued.

Reverting to baby talk the old woman asked, "What's your name then?"

Bouncing on his mother's lap the now smiling toddler's face lit up.

"He's called Josh."

"Arh Joshua."

"No Josh. His father's Joshua." corrected the mother. Then looking towards the buggy, she continued.

"And there's Rose fast asleep there."

"Don't tell me, not short for Rosemary." Laughed the old woman.

"I'm Rosemary."

"'Ow do you do Rosemary. I'm Vi, short for Violet." Both women giggled.

"Yeah, as I was saying, I used to be all to everyone. When my kids went to school I was a care assistant and worked all God's hours. Then when I got home, I'd look after Bert, my hubby, and the kids. When they grew up and left, it was just me an' Bert. Then he got sick and died. I just carried on working. Oh, I did a bit of voluntary at the old people's home as well. I 'ated being in on mi own, so I just carried on and on 'til I was under the doctor with mi nerves. They call it breakdown, or depression these days. Anyway, I ended up in 'ospital for months and months. You never guess what they said it was – all that work and looking after other people. No one could've looked after them better than me! Anyway, they said I didn't look after miself. Fancy that? Like I had the time!

Take my advice. As much as you love them kiddies, hubby, and anyone else, you gotta look after yurself. You're impor'ant too.

Oop. This is my stop. Take care. Bye. Bye Josh."

Josh attempted the wave and Rosemary responded, "Thanks for the advice. Take care. Bye."

Violet retrieved her four wheeled shopping trolley and carefully stepped off the bus.

Some years later, Rosemary gave Violet's advice to her daughter-in- law, as she, a mother of twins, had confided that she was feeling overwhelmed.

Self –Reflection

Self –Reflection

Nightmare

- What did you think was 'wrong' with Emma?
- Were you surprised? If so, why?
- Are you aware that some people with mental illness/emotional stress are mistreated in a similar way to Emma?

Been there!

- If you've experienced mental illness/ emotional stress, how was it for you?
- How were you supported?
- What have you learnt from your experience?
- How are you now?
- What are you doing now?

The Unlikely Samaritan

- Have you looked after someone who has experienced mental illness/emotional stress?

- How was it for you?

- How were you supported?

The Valuable Advice

- What is the learning from this story?

*

- What is the moral of these stories?

- Have you changed your perception of those with mental illness/emotional stress?

Those with mental illness, an unseen condition, should receive the same support and compassion as having a headache, another unseen condition – the same support and compassion as someone with a broken leg would receive!

NOTES

For advice & information contact:

RETHINK MENTAL ILLNESS

on:

Telephone: 0300 5000 927 (10am-2pm Monday to Friday)
Email: info@rethink.org
Website: http://www.rethink.org/about-us/our-mental-health-advice

*

MIND

on:

Telephone: 0300 123 3393
Telephone: 0300 123 3393 (9am-5pm Monday to Friday)
Email: info@mind.org.uk
Website: www.mind.org.uk/help/advice_lines

SANE

on:

Telephone: 0845 767 8000
Telephone: 0845 767 8000 (6pm-11pm)
Website: www.sane.org.uk/what_we_do/support /helpline

*

SAMARITANS

on:

Tel: 08457 90 90 90 (24 hours a day)
Email: jo@samaritans.org
Website: www.samaritans.org

www.ingramcontent.com/pod-product-compliance
Ingram Content Group UK Ltd.
Pitfield, Milton Keynes, MK11 3LW, UK
UKHW020228250726
13967UKWH00001B/245

9 781291 717686